Flipping Houses: The Road to Millions

What EVERY Beginner Needs to Know

Table Of Contents

Introduction 3

Chapter 1: Understanding What House Flipping Is 5

Chapter 2: Financing 13

Chapter 3: Finding a Property 19

Chapter 4: The Work Itself 29

Chapter 5: Selling Your Flip 35

Chapter 6: The Formula Behind Flipping 45

Conclusion 56

Introduction

I want to thank you and congratulate you for ordering the book "Flipping Houses: The Road to Millions (What EVERY Beginner Needs to Know)."

This book has proven steps and strategies on how to become a truly accomplished flipper. You'll want to take advantage of these tips and strategies instead of heading into your first flip "blind," especially if you're entering into this business in hopes of making money. There are definitely some things you'll want to know and understand in this regard.

With this in mind, here's an inescapable fact: You will need this book to guide you through the flipping process, especially your very first flip. There are many things you need to know, from the first step of buying your first property, through rehabbing it and finally selling it. Everything you need to know is right here for you.

If you do not develop your flipping plan, you won't make millions. As such, we've outlined the steps to every part of your flip. From investing in a property to rehabbing it, and finally selling it for a profit. Everything you need to know is right here in this book for you.

Additionally, the art of Flipping Houses is only one component of the multi-faceted approach that falls under the broad spectrum of Real Estate Investing. Our books tackle all these other components in detail as well. To name just a few other topics that a successful Real Estate Investor should strive to understand, we have Rental Property Investing, Real Estate Sales with details on how to embark on a career as a successful Real Estate Agent, and even a step by step guide to achieving an excellent Credit Score to get you the loan with the best rates. And for anyone interested in the Tiny House Movement, we have books on that subject as well!!

You can find books on all of these topics- AND MORE- by visiting our Amazon Author Page at the following link: https://www.amazon.com/-/e/B01LYIFPLO

While this guide to Flipping Houses will provide a detailed technical analysis of the science behind the Flip, our other books will focus much more in depth on Real Estate Investing in general. If you check out our Real Estate Library, you are guaranteed to profit from Real Estate, Rental Properties, Flipping Houses, and turn this into a lucrative income stream for the rest of your life. Don't miss out!!

With all that being said, let's dive into the meat and potatoes of this book. It's time for you to become an amazing flipper.

Chapter 1:
Understanding What House Flipping Is

Flipping: The act of buying a house then reselling it for a profit.

Although today's real estate market is still somewhat depressed, there's big money found in flipping houses. This is nothing more than simple economics: Buy low, sell high. You're sole intent is to buy a house and turn a profit with the highest rate possible and as fast as possible. In other words, you should never look at this as a long-term investment.

Unfortunately, you can't guarantee you'll see a profit when you flip a house because quite often you don't know what lies behind the walls until you actually buy the house. However, there are some things you can do to pad yourself along the way:

- Make sure you have liquid capital available for when something unforeseen happens.

- By keeping your day job you'll have stability and won't overstep your financial boundaries.

- Make sure you check out the deal for yourself. Don't pay for anything you haven't seen in person.

- Don't be lured in by the idea of fast cash.

- Never take on too much property at once because this will over extend your financial position, which is something you don't want to do.

There are various strategies used in flipping houses today. Each has its own advantages and disadvantages, giving you the opportunity to earn some extra money and the opportunity to build a profitable, long-term business.

Deciding if Flipping is for You: The pros and Cons

Not to scare you, but you really need to look at the pros and cons of flipping before you enter into this business. It's important you understand that while this is an easy, glamorous way of investing money and building wealth, there's still risk involved and you need to know that entering into this process.

With this in mind, let's first look at the cons, which include:

- The "Bubble Burst" is when there's a drop in real estate prices either at the national or local level. Typically, a higher supply than there is demand for housing causes this to occur. There are several reasons for this including increasing interest rates, increased lending rules, or local developers over-building in an area. New, extreme tax increases, and increasing crime rates often cause sudden drops in the value of real estate, making houses difficult or impossible to sell.

- You're always faced with the potential of losing money. While flipping is oftentimes a very profitable, short-term investment, if you don't properly budget your money and make room for both accounting mistakes and time delays, you could make a lot less money than you'd expected, break even, or lose money.

- It's also possible for you to over commit yourself. In the beginning, you'll probably think you can do more of the work yourself than is actually possible. Be realistic about the entire process or you'll seriously impair your budget and the overall project too. Often, this is the difference between making and losing money on a flip.

Now for the positive side of things, the pros include:

- There aren't many investments that will give you a crash course in budgeting faster than flipping will. You must learn to budget quickly if you want to profit from your flip. Otherwise, you'll watch yourself losing your profit. Here you mustn't only create a budget, but you have to stick to it. This is a vital skill for any successful flipper. Of course, this will also help you with your finances in other areas of your life as well.

- You'll greatly benefit from learning how to pay attention to details. This is a skill that will grow with each flip you do. It's important because you make or break your profit in your flip's small details. Potential buyers look for these things because it shows you care for your property.

- Watch as your credit rating grows exponentially. This will make it easier for you to borrow money in the future since banks look at loans you take out and pay back. By profiting on a flip, the bank grows more willing to lend you more money (a.k.a. increase your borrowing power) for your next flip. This is why if you can only start small, you should still get started and grow from there.

- The better you are at adapting to changes, the more successful you'll be at flipping houses. This is important because in business things change fast, even overnight.

When these changes hit, it's important for you to change or update your business strategy so your success continues. This is also true with the techniques you learn along the way for rehabbing houses because what works for one house may not work for the next house.

Successfully flipping a house has the potential for a high yield investment. This can happen in a relatively short amount of time too. Of course, as with any high yield investment, flipping isn't without its risks. Therefore, you must carefully weigh both the pros and cons before you get involved with house flipping.

Types of Flipping

Essentially, there are two types of flipping:

- Wholesaling is when you buy a property and immediately resell it for a profit. You don't do any major repair or maintenance so you don't put up any money for the house. It's important you're a strong negotiator or this won't work. You must convince a seller to sell their property at well-below market value then convince the buyer to pay you near market value money.

- Rehabbing is when you buy property that's in disrepair, fix it up, then sell it. You can choose to focus on houses that need some minor repairs or tackle larger projects (e.g. houses with structural problems, fire damage, water damage).

The Cost of Flipping

One of the biggest questions on most people's minds is, "How much am I earn flipping houses?" There aren't any correct answers here since part-time flippers won't make as much as part-time flippers. Additionally, where you live plays a big role in how much a house sells for. However, if you manage one or two flips per month on your own you could average $40,000. So, over the course of a year, you could average between $240K and $480K. Obviously, the more flips you handle each month, the more money you'll make.

Taxes

Don't forget you have to pay taxes on your profits, though. "Profits" are defined as any money left from when you sell a house, minus your rehab costs (including labor and materials) and your fixed costs (e.g. commissions, fees, closing costs, loans, taxes, insurance, utilities). You're taxed at the same percentage as if you worked a full-time job. As such, they significantly eat into your profit margin. Once you're sure you're serious about flipping, make sure you consult a CPA who can help you structure your business so you pay the least amount of taxes possible.

8 Things you Must Know Before Starting Your First Flip

So, you think you're ready to get started with your first house flip? Well, before you do so it's important that you "know what you're doing." There are ways in which you can avoid losing money or spending too much of it when you're completing your first flip. With this in mind, here are the top 8 things you really should know before flipping your first house:

- Make sure you actually know what you're doing. You can't jump into the house flipping business blindly. While you don't need real estate experience to flip a house, you do need to make sure you maximize the time and money you invest into this business. Some of the things you must know include how to find funding; how to find, negotiate and close a great deal; what materials are popular; what high price items you should invest in; what low-cost materials you can use; how to hire inexpensive contractors; how to manage contractors, ensuring they meet your timeline; how to market your property properly; how to make the highest profit.

- Learn how to analyze a real estate deal. One of the biggest mistakes first-time flippers make is during this step. It's not easy to create a really sound investment. This is something you'll learn throughout your first deal.

- Never fudge your repair costs even if you're optimistic. When you have a complete inspection in the beginning, you may think you can make your budget really tight, but you never know when unforeseen issues may pop up. Even the most highly experienced flipper will tell you that you can never project too high of repair costs. As such, it's important you take a rational look at your repair costs.

- Never grow emotionally attached to your flip. Extravagance has no room here. You're working for profit. As such, you should only spend money on things that make sense, not the things you'd want if you were moving into the house (because you're not). It's important your choices are data driven. This is something you must thoroughly understand before starting your flip.

- Don't rationalize things. Stick to your original ARV. While temptation will arise, you shouldn't give into it ever. You also can't count on the market consistently appreciating. When a shift occurs, if you ignore your original ARV, you'll eliminate any room you had for profit.

- The faster you finish your flip and sell your house, the faster you pay back your loan and earn your profit to invest in your next flip. Things like hiring contractors, getting them to finish your project on time and selling your house are the most time-consuming aspects of your flip. This is why it's so important for you to know how to manage the project from the beginning to the end. Make sure you're comfortable negotiating and managing projects. These things play a vital role in making sure you earn the amount of money you want.

- It's important you know what's selling in your flip's neighborhood and why. You also need to know what buyers are expecting from those houses, as well as what's trending. The best way of accomplishing this is through online research and slowly driving through the neighborhood, looking at the other houses there.

- Never leave your contractors unsupervised. You also can't simply trust they're giving you reasonable prices. Instead, you must check on your contractors regularly and know what you should expect them to charge you for their time and materials. When contractors are unscrupulous they not only prolong the time it takes for you to sell the home, but they also cut into your profit margin because you'll have to pay more interest and take longer between flips. For these reasons, you must learn how to supervise and manage your contractors, keeping them on your timeline, not theirs.

While being an expert isn't necessary for you to start flipping houses, you do need to keep these things in mind. Throughout your firs flip you'll feel a mix of stress and excitement. It's during this time you'll learn enough to feel comfortable and confident with your next flip. Remember, knowledge is power and with the help of this book, there's no reason you can't have a successful first flip.

Chapter 2: Financing

Before you can flip a house, you must own the property first. This is where you'll need good credit so you can qualify for one of the following types of real estate financing. However, if you don't have good credit now, don't worry: There are still some ways you can buy your first property and enter the flipping business.

Conventional Financing

A mortgage broker or a large banking institution does this. They base your ability to qualify for a loan strictly on your current financial situation (e.g. credit score, income, assets, debt). Without good credit, reasonable income, and a low amount of debt, you probably won't qualify for this type of financing, but don't feel bad since most people won't qualify for it either.

While lenders offer low-interest rates, low loan costs, and a long loan duration for conventional financing, it's difficult to get because investors don't lend against properties that aren't move-in ready. For this reason, most lenders take a long time to appraise a house (usually 21 days) and if they're financing through Freddie Mac or Fannie Mae, which most do, you're limited to 4 – 10 loans at one time.

Portfolio/Investor Loans

Small banks (ones with only 3 – 5 branches) lend their own money, hence they're known as "portfolio lenders." As such, they choose who they want to loan to, but your financial situation doesn't matter as long as you don't have a bankruptcy, foreclosure, or any large unpaid debts on your credit. They'll take your real estate experience and the type of deal you're seeking into consideration, though. With this said, if they feel you have a solid investment, you'll more than likely receive financing.

Typically, you must put down less than 30% down payment with these loans. Some of these will even offer you a "rehab loan," meaning they roll the rehab costs into your loan. In either case, they're mostly concerned in making sure you're about to make a sound investment. Since they're highly accustomed to doing this, they can usually close your loan in 7 – 10 days.

Most portfolio loans are short-term (6 – 12 months), so it's important you're confident so you can finish the property and sell it in that amount of time. However, considering these loans usually have higher interest rates, it's in your best interest to complete the loan as soon as possible anyway. Also, remember the lender is very interested in your deal and will seriously scrutinize it. This is why they'll usually want to see that you have real estate experience.

Private Investors

These are well-off professionals (e.g. doctors, lawyers, business professionals) who have money (cash or retirement funds) to invest who expect better returns than what they'd receive from the stock market or other such venues, usually by about 8 - 12%. Usually, you already know these people so you can approach them easily.

This is great if you can prove your ability to find and execute real estate deals, these investors typically don't care about your creditworthiness. However, it can take a lot of work to convince these people to trust you with their money because they usually don't have much experience with real estate. This is why you need a good business plan, a track record of being a hard worker, and trustworthiness.

Hard Money Lenders

A hard money-lender (a.k.a. HML) loans against the property's value instead of against you, the borrower. Typically, they pool funds from wealthy people then lend the money to you at a high rate. These are good loans for new investors with little cash or experience because you can get them quickly.

While these loans are available, regardless of your financial situation, there are some definite drawbacks. For instance, they'll often charge you a higher lending rate. You must consider whether the money is worth the charges, but there are times when a HML will lend you 100% of both the purchase and rehab costs. However, considering the interest rates, which are usually 15% or more, this can eat up your profit margin rather quickly.

Equity Investors

These lenders will lend you money in return for a fixed percentage of the investment and the profit. They're more commonly known as a "partner with cash" because while you do all the work, ultimately you split the profit and only receive 50% of it as they take the other 50%. The nice thing is there are no "requirements" for you to fulfill so you can receive a loan since you're usually working with a friend or family member.

Besides the fact the lender takes 50% of your profit, another drawback to working with an equity investor is they typically want to take an active role in your investment. This is good only if they're experienced and share in your vision. Otherwise, it's usually a recipe for disaster.

Choosing the Right Type of Financing

When you're ready to check on which of these investors is a good fit for you, prepare yourself to have the following 5 key components of your financial resume scrutinized:

- Make sure you know your credit history and score. These numbers are important for getting your deals funded. You want a score of at least 680 or you'll find yourself immediately dismissed from consideration.

- Assets such as cash in the bank, stocks, bonds, large retirement accounts, property ownership, and investment properties all make your lender feel more comfortable working with you. This is because these things are usable when it's time to collateralize against your loan. However, be aware that if you can't repay your loan, the lender gets your collateral.

- Large amounts of debt make it difficult for you to get financing because lenders feel it will impede upon your ability to repay your loan. However, if you have a lot of debt (e.g. rent/mortgage, monthly bills, etc.) in comparison to your income, then you have a better chance of getting a loan with a low-interest rate (ideally, under 30%).

- Large amounts of debt make it difficult for you to get financing because lenders feel it will impede upon your ability to repay your loan. However, if you have a lot of debt (e.g. rent/mortgage, monthly bills, etc.) in comparison to your income, then you have a better chance of getting a loan with a low-interest rate (ideally, under 30%).

- Investing experience is also of concern to some lenders because those with a long investment history are much less of a risk than inexperienced investors. If you're inexperienced, a good business plan is sometimes a good substitute as it shows you have a well thought out plan and clear direction.

Flipping When You Have no Money

If you're like most aspiring investors today, you don't have any cash, credit, or money. This isn't something that should stop you, though. Instead, spend some time searching for another investor to partner with or either a HML or private lender.

When you do find someone who is willing to lend you money, it's important you know these tips for successful borrowing:

- They'll look at your credit score to decide if you're credit worthy. This is why you shouldn't borrow too much money and always repay what you owe on time.

- Make sure you understand the interest rate (the amount you're charged for borrowing money) and the loan's terms. Look for things like statements saying they'll charge you a penalty rate for prepaying your loan or there are late fees if your loan isn't paid by a certain time each month.

- Think carefully about how much money you borrow. Since you're charged an interest rate, you'll ultimately end up paying back more money. This is why you don't want to borrow more money than you need or can afford.

- The application process requires you give your lender various types of information (e.g. credit score, proof of income). You'll want to know what information to take with you when you're applying for a loan, especially if you need the money immediately.

- Know what the repayment period (how long you have to repay your loan) is. The shorter the repayment period, the less interest you'll pay, but this also requires you pay slightly more on your loan.

- Have a plan for repaying the loan before borrowing the money.

Chapter 3:
Finding a Property

Knowing how to borrow money is important. Armed with that knowledge and ability, you'll want to start looking at houses. One of the most common ways of doing this is by finding a Realtor, but a few other methods exist and are worth mentioning as well.

Budgeting for Your First Flip

Decisions you make about the house you're flipping, either before or during the project, can and will affect the size of your profit. This is why it's so important you create a budget for your whole project, not just the purchasing and rehabbing prices, and then stick to it.

With this in mind, here's a checklist you can use while creating the budget for your first flip:

- You must start by determining the after repair value (ARV) of your flip. This is what you can base your expected ROI upon once you've placed the house on the market. A trusted Realtor will help you choose your property's estimated ARV.

- Rehab costs vary greatly depending on the house you buy and how much rehab work it needs. Make sure you track all the house's necessary repairs. This will make you much more knowledgeable when it comes time for your next flip.

- Financing and carrying costs are easy to overlook, but make sure you don't. These costs include your loan, as well as paying for things until you sell the house. Some of the items you can't afford to overlook and which fall into this category include financing loan(s), property taxes, utilities (e.g. gas, water, electric), property insurance, and sometimes you'll also need to pay HOA or condo fees. You should also note that the longer your rehab work takes, as well as the amount of time your post-rehab house remains on the market, the higher your carrying costs will be. This will diminish your flip's profit too.

- Realtor fees are also involved because while you can sell your flip yourself if you want the fastest turnaround time on your investment and the biggest profit, you should hire a good real estate agent. Not only are they worth their commission fee, but they'll also help you save money on your flip in the long run.

- Some of the other costs that often get overlooked include inspection fees, interest on loans, contingencies, and closing costs.

Typically, you can break your average budget down into the following cost percentages:

- 53.25% of your budget will go towards the house's buying price

- 20% of your budget will pay for labor

- 6.5% of your budget will pay for materials

- 8% of your budget will pay for carrying costs, utilities, commissions, and other hidden fees

- 12.25% will result in profit

Realistic budgeting is the key to reduced risk. Of course, there's nothing that will cut the inherent risks associated with house flipping, but creating a realistic budget will most definitely help mitigate at least some of your risk. Another way in which you can "manage" some of these risks is by becoming as thoroughly knowledgeable in the realm of house flipping as you can before making your first investment. Also, make sure you always follow the old saying, "Never invest more than you can afford to lose."

Finding a Realtor

Since you don't want just any Realtor, there are some things you'll want to do so you learn more about this person before hiring them:

- Talk with clients to find out what the Realtor's asking price is, what type of house they, how long their house was on the market, and how they felt about their experience.

- Contact the state licensing board to see if they're in good standing.

- Find out if they've ever won the "Realtor of the Year" award by the state or local branch of the National Association of Realtors (NAR). These are Realtors whose peers voted them "the best."

- Check out their credentials and specialties (what areas they have special training in). There are many of these credentials, including CRS (Certified Residential Specialist) completed training in handling residential real estate; ABR (Accredited Buyer's Representative) completed training buyer representation, and SRES (Seniors Real Estate Specialist) completed training in helping senior citizens.

- Learn how long the agent has been in business. You want someone with over 5 years experience and who specializes in the neighborhood and price range your flip is in.

- Review their current listings. Make sure they're effectively using the Internet since this is where most people begin their search. This is another opportunity for you to see if they're selling properties like yours. It's also important the Realtor has plenty of listings without having so many you become just a number to them.

- Find out what other houses are for sale near yours. Your Realtor should be able to tell you about them without having to look the information up. If they have to go searching for the information, they don't really know their properties.

Finding a Realtor with these qualifications may take some work, but it's well worth it. With them by your side, it's time to find your first house to flip. You'll need to put some thought into this as well. Although you don't plan on living here, this is still important because it affects your investment's value.

The Importance of Your Flip's Location

Understanding your location's importance, here's what you should think about:

- Geographic location: What part of the country do you want to flip houses in? Things like house prices, job opportunities, and good schools are important.

- City vs. suburbs vs. rural: What setting is best? Here you must consider how much peace and quiet is important, how big of lot size you need, and how close you want your property located to things people want and need.

- Neighborhood: What characteristics are important to you here? You'll want a place where people feel comfortable, have good schools, and stores nearby. People will pay more to live in a good neighborhood with good schools and where the overall neighborhood is safe so they don't continually need to watch their backs.

- You should also visit the property during the day and again at night. Neighborhoods don't typically appear the same on paper as they do when you're in them. Little details (e.g. narrow streets, cars parked on the street) often make a huge difference. It's also important to understand neighborhoods may feel comfortable throughout the day then feel disconcerting at night. The same is true of neighborhoods during different types of weather.

Once you know what factors are most important to you about location, you need to research some neighborhoods, especially if you're not already familiar with these locations. You can easily find all kinds of facts and statistics online. However, it's also a good idea to talk to the neighborhood's current residents and local police department to get more information.

All of these things clearly affect your flip's renovation potential. Another important thing that influences this is how much work the house really needs and whether you can do it. According to Jeff Beneke, author of "The Fence Bible," you want to make sure it's possible to close off one part of a house at a time when you're turning it into an apartment building. This allows you to "close off one room at a time, do what you have to do in that, move somebody into there, then close off another room" and keep working.

Buying Your First Flip

When you find jobs you don't feel comfortable doing yourself, it's important to get estimates on the cost of that work before buying the property. If the cost of this work places the house at a higher value than others in the neighborhood, it's not a good investment unless you can somehow scale back the other renovations.

While it's important to "pretend you're living there," you shouldn't allow these pretty, clean properties to romance you. This isn't what you're getting into. Instead, take a few moments to:

- Try everything in the house (e.g. flush the toilets, turn on the lights, climb the stairs, check the water flow in the showers and sinks)

- Look up at the ceiling instead of only looking at floors and walls because then you'll know if there's any water damage.

Think Long-Term

You'll want to keep these things in mind as you look at the various types of properties available for you to buy today. They include:

- Distressed properties are houses whose owners aren't maintaining and thus they're either neglected or in poor condition. The price of such houses is usually well below market value, making them very interesting to many flippers. However, the main risk is the house's condition.

- Commercial property includes stores, offices, warehouses, hotels, malls, farms, apartment buildings, and garages. These have income potential so typically you'll see a 6 – 12% annual return off your buying price. At the same time, you'll also receive a more objective price evaluation. However, these properties take a lot of time, regardless how many tenants or business owners occupy the property. As such, you'll need professional help with these types of properties, right from the beginning since they need a larger initial investment too. This makes everything much riskier.

- Foreclosed properties are ones in which the lender is trying to recover the loan's balance from a borrower who's stopped making payments. This often allows you to buy a better house or one in a better neighborhood. It's also financially advantageous since you pay less than market value. Unfortunately, these houses are typically overdue for house repairs including mold buildup, broken pipes, vermin, and bug infestations.

Finding the Best Deal

Regardless what type of property you choose to buy, you should always watch for the best deal. Some ways of finding these deals include:

- Drive around a neighborhood you like and find a house you think needs some work. Once you find a distressed or vacant property, write down its address and any notes, even a few photos. With this house dig into the public records or do a reverse phone number search, then write a letter offering to buy the property.

- Send out direct mail (a large number of targeted letters or postcards) to people who may want to sell their house. This sometimes seems like shooting in the dark, but if you send out 1,000 letters and 5% of the recipients (50 people) call for more information, then 5% of these folks sell you their house, you'll buy 2 houses. As such, this is actually money well spent.

- Target landlords going through evictions because this is a stressful, expensive time that makes many of them question whether they want to continue in this business. You can find them by looking through your county's public record.

- Conduct an online search. Look through various forums and on Craigs List. In doing so, you'll want to search for sellers, post ads, and search for landlords. When searching for landlords, you want to avoid professional property management companies. Instead, call up the other landlords, explain you want to invest in real estate in that area and wondered if they'd consider selling you their property. Even if they don't want to sell their property, they probably know someone who wants to sell theirs.

- Get deals from wholesalers, which are people who find great deals on real estate, contract them, then sell them to another investor for slightly more money. Make sure you only work with good ones or consider training someone to do this work for you.

Your House's Contract

After you use one of these methods to find a property to buy, you're on to the contract. It's essential you understand the contract and that it meets your expectations. Typically, the language used in it is relatively easy to understand.

Nonetheless, you must still move forward with caution since it's legally binding and misinterpretation can cost a lot of money.

With this in mind, make sure you:

- Consult a real estate dictionary so you can understand any unfamiliar terms.

- Read the contract thoroughly, checking for accuracy about the property's location, price, down payment, financing, closing date, and contingencies.

- See the seller's responsibilities clear defined.

- Have a warranty clause obligating the seller to give you a clear title.

- Verify the contract's details, which should include what happens to your good-faith deposit if the transaction isn't completed, as well as provisions for an inspection and a final walk-through before closing.

- Carefully note the precise conditions for contract withdrawal terms.

- Talk to a real estate attorney if anything isn't clear. While this costs a fee, it's important you make sure everything is clear before signing a contract.

Chapter 4:
The Work Itself

While a range of 20 – 30% of a house's value is an acceptable amount to invest in renovations, this is only true when you plan on living there for 10 or more years. Since you're flipping the house, you really only should invest 15 – 20% of its value in its remodel.

Over Rehabbing and Under Rehabbing

It's important to understand you can also over or under rehab a property. You must keep things reasonable, especially if you're dealing with distressed properties, under market value. Aim for buying a house at 20% under market value, doing some light rehab then reselling it for a 12% annual return on investment (ROI). Of course, the level of rehab depends on the house's location. Overdoing a rehab causes your ROI to plummet. Of course, not doing enough rehab, especially in a really nice neighborhood, means the house will sit and sit.

Choosing What to Rehab

To decide what to repair on a house, look at the other houses in the neighborhood. Look at what materials they used and their quality. Typically, the more expensive a neighborhood, the better you should make your rehab.

While you're not using your money on the flip, you must pay back any money you've borrowed so you don't want to over borrow. Regardless what you pay up front, the most important number is your after repair value (ARV). You can figure this out by knowing what you can sell the property for when you're finished flipping it. Do this by accessing the MLS, which allows you to compare the other houses like yours that sold in the past 6 months. If no other houses have sold, there may be no demand for the type of house you're selling. Also, look at what Realtors priced these houses at. With this number in mind, you can start deciding what you should pay for the various costs associated with your flip.

Knowing When to Stop

After spending some time flipping houses you'll eventually run into one that's a total flop. Regardless how much research you did on the property and its neighborhood, along with the time you invested in finding great deals, you'll still run across a few of these types of houses.

How do you know when you've reached the point where you simply can't do anything more for a house? There are four ways you'll know when it's time to stop. They include:

- Take a look at what the house needs in comparison to your rehab budget. While some houses look great from the outside, you'll find structural damage or leaky ceilings when you go inside. Things like this threaten to take up your entire rehab budget and turn what looks like a great flip into a major nightmare. This is when you need to step back and decide how much work you can do and how much work you need the professionals to do for you. Thinking this through will help you shave some money off so you stay in your budget. However, don't waste a lot of time here because you're losing money. So, if you think the professionals can do the work better and faster, you probably should just let them go ahead and do the work for you.

- Don't get involved with a flip that needs structural repairs unless you have "deep pockets." This is why your contractors should take a really good look at the entire house before you start doing anything. Structural damage will quickly eat up your whole budget so instead of investing all your money in this, step back and consider what you'll need to do to get the house in living condition. If that's not possible, then you'll have to consider demolishing the entire house and starting all over again.

- Put your rehab tasks in order of importance. Make the house's exterior first on your list so you can get a "for sale" sign up on it fast. For this, you need to make the home look good because curb appeal makes the first, and most vital, impression. Of course, you don't want to start showing your house while contractors are still working on it. This generates interest in the home while you're working on it. You can then use this interest to gauge how much work you can afford to do.

- Remember the main principle of flipping is getting the house in the best shape possible for its market so you can make a really good profit for yourself. Now, this doesn't mean you should do poor quality work, but this principle should help guide you as you decide what you need to do to bring the home up to market value and sell it as quickly as possible.

They call this process "flipping" for a reason. It's because the sooner you get the house into great shape while remaining within your budget, the sooner you'll see a return on your investment and be ready to move on to your next flip. So, if a little detail here or there isn't going to do anything to improve the house's value, then don't do it. It's time to sell the house instead.

Don't Overlook Financing Costs

Here you need to ask your Realtor how long other houses in your neighborhood have sat on the market. Your Realtor should also be able to give you his thoughts on why some houses are selling while others aren't. It's important you only borrow as much money as you need for buying and flipping the house, but don't forget you also have other bills to pay along the way too (e.g. electric bill, gas bill, water bill, insurance, lawn mowing, property taxes).

When you break this down to numbers, it may look something like this:

- You get a $120,000 loan at 10% interest meaning your annual interest is $12,000 ($120,000 x 10% = $12,000)

- You spend four months renovating the house, which then sits on the market for a month and closing takes a month so you pay 6 months of interest or $6,000

Obviously, your biggest cost is the renovation itself, especially since you don't want to get involved in unethical "fix and flips." Instead, you want to do high-quality work while maintaining healthy profit margins. Of course, you don't have to do any of this work yourself. There are many different types of contractors available for you to choose from today, including:

- A really good handyman can tackle many of the different parts of your rehab for you (e.g. carpentry, sheet-rock, basic electrical, basic plumbing, basic HVAC).

- A general contractor is basically a licensed handyman, but he can also hire and pay subcontractors. This allows him to have more time for handling scheduling and the budget.

- Contractors are different from a general contractor. If you choose to use them without hiring a general contractor, it's important you're much more hands on in scheduling and managing them. The county you live in licenses and insures contractors in the area they specialize in. Some of the most well-known contractors include Terminex (pest/termite) and Roto Rooter (plumbing).

Your goal is to have these people in place the day you close on the property so you can start working right away. This is also the day you want all the utilities switched over into your name and turned on. The project's success relies on you, ultimately. As such, you have to keep on top of everything. Ask questions, know what's going on at all times, and visit the job site as often as possible to keep everything on schedule.

When using a general contractor, make sure to outline how and when you'll distribute all the draws (a payment made to the contractor for work that's been completed). There are some guidelines you should follow here:

- The first draw should happen at the beginning of the project before starting any work. With this draw, your contractor can buy the necessary materials for starting the work. Make sure this isn't more than 25% of the project's total cost, though.

- Make more draws at agreed upon "milestones" (when they've completed specific jobs).

- At the end of the flip, make sure you're happy with everything before making the last draw.

Sometimes extra or unexpected issues arise costing you money. If you're not careful, this can really blow your budget and eat away at your ROI. While you should expect things to come up, make sure you're in control of approving them before they spend any money. This way you can carefully check it instead of just agreeing because the contractor said so. It's your job to ask questions so you truly understand what they're spending the money on.

Always remember, this is your project, you are in control. This is why being on premises regularly is so important. However, you should remember that you're not there to work or run errands for anyone. It's your contractor's job to manage the project, get the materials, and coordinate the subcontractors. You're there to look at the work's quality as it's done so you can point out any issues as soon as you see them. In doing so you'll feel more comfortable tactfully pointing out things that you must fix, instead of presenting your contractor with a long list of items. Of course, this also makes your general contractor more aware that you're on top of things and that you actually pay attention to details. In turn, this will make him more conscious of the details as well.

Chapter 5:
Selling Your Flip

Since you've already managed all the house flipping work, you may think you can now manage the sale of the house yourself as well. However, you should know that the money you'd spend on commissions is typically a wash when you consider the cost of hiring an experienced Realtor. This is because most houses that are "for sale by owner" (FSBO) take longer to sell and then when they do sell, they typically sell for less money.

Reasons to Hire a Realtor

If the money wasn't enough of an incentive for hiring a Realtor, here are some other really good reasons for doing so:

- This is a major business transaction which includes three important negotiations along the way: the initial offer, followed by the counter offer, then once everyone reaches an agreement, there's the post-offer (e.g. inspections, requests for concessions).

- It's important your house receive as much exposure as possible in front of lots of potential buyers. Your Realtor prepares all the marketing.

- materials, coordinates the online marketing, hosts open houses, and networks with other agents who have potential buyers.

- A Realtor typically represents most buyers. They're usually deterred by an FSBO because they're afraid the won't receive their commission.

- The process is smoother because Realtors know how to efficiently work their way through the sales process.

For Sale by Owner

Of course, if you're dead set on selling the house yourself, you should know there are some benefits to doing this as well. They include:

- You pay yourself instead of paying an agent commission.

- Since your house probably doesn't have much equity, you may end up paying some of the Realtor's commission yourself. You can avoid this with a FSBO and thus you'll lose money.

- You'll still have work to do when you work with a Realtor (e.g. repairs, cleaning, staging). Then when you do find a buyer the two of you will need to figure out how to pay the Realtor's commission. So, while a FSBO is a lot of work, you'll receive a great payout for doing so, especially considering you won't lose money in any of these ways.

- When you do have a FSBO you'll have expenses like the cost of an appraisal, running ads in your local newspaper, and hiring a lawyer to oversee the contract. However, you're in control of these things yourself with a FSBO. You'll also want to learn how to stage your house since you won't have anyone to do it for you.

Staging Your Flip for a Faster Sale

Staging is the act of preparing your house for sale. Your goal is to make your house look truly appealing to most people so you can quickly sell it for more money. You also want to help your potential buyer envision themselves living in the house. With this in mind, here are some things you should do:

- Arrange each room to showcase its purpose.

- Make sure the rooms are all painted in neutral colors.

- Scrub the floors.

- Deodorize the house so there are no nasty smells.

- Bake fresh-baked cookies to serve or boil cinnamon sticks on the stove before each showing.

- Don't forget about enhancing curb appeal! Since this is the buyer's first impression, it's somewhat more important than cleaning the inside of the house. So, mow the lawn and pick up any trash.

Having Your Flip Appraised

All of these things will help with your house's appraisal as well. This is a professional's "educated guess" (opinion) of the size, condition, function and quality of your house. A credible financial institution won't lend a buyer money for a house until they've conducted an appraisal. This is because the bank wants to know what the loan collateral will sell for in a worst-case scenario," says Bart Jackson, an appraiser, and Realtor with Charleston Preferred Properties in Charleston, South

Carolina. They don't want stuck with a house they lent a buyer money for only to discover it's not worth its buying price.

This is how the appraisal process works... When they arrive on your property they will:

- Inspect your house

- Research the value of other houses in your neighborhood to see what they're selling at and arrive at a fair market value.

- Provide you with a final report which includes all their data and research, as well as their final "opinion of value."

Real estate attorney Robert Pellegrini from Bridgewater, Massachusetts issues a word of caution about this process in that if your appraisal comes in under purchase price, most buyers will have room in their contract to end or renegotiate the contract. This is why it's best for both parties to get this appraisal, but you, the seller, is the one who must pay for it at the time of closing. Typically, this will cost up to several hundreds of dollars.

Having Your Flip Appraised

This appraisal is different from your house inspection, which is also necessary. Inspectors usually arrive before appraisers and are there to look for any defects in the house that would cost the buyer money later on. Of course, if an appraiser notices a problem they will point it out to the inspector and vice versa.

The appraisal process typically takes a week or two. This is because underwriters can ask for more information and pictures of the house than in the past. There really isn't anything you can do to move this process along, but staging your house and having a list of all the repairs (nothing formal or detailed, just a list) you've done to it are both beneficial. If you have a Realtor, they'll meet the appraiser at the house to share this list, and any other pertinent information, with them. Your Realtor can also give the appraiser other information, including that on comparable houses to justify your house's selling price.

Having Your Flip Inspected

As stated before, the inspector arrives later in the process and is different from the appraiser. They're the ones who really take a close, deep look at your house to see if there are any "hidden" issues. You don't only want to hire one after you've rehabbed a house, but some people will encourage you to hire one before buying one too. This is because they can tell you a lot about the property's condition. Of course, you can also become really good at this job and do it yourself.

Some things a good inspector will look for include looking for:

- Any sign of mold, water leakages, cracks or leaks in the foundation, rotting wooden beams in the basement, as well as ensuring that the plumbing systems should also be in good working order

- Moisture and cracks in the crawl space, if one exists

- Evidence of water leakage or damage in the attic

- Sufficient insulation for your area of the country

- Leaks, water stains, and mildew, as well as water pressure and proper drainage in the bathroom and kitchen plumbing

- Easy access to the main breaker box or fuse box, that's in good condition

- A sufficient number of electrical outlets

- Ground fault circuit interrupters (a.k.a. GFCI) to prevent shock from occurring in both the kitchen and the bathroom

- An appropriately sized HVAC system

- Shingles - accounted for and in good condition

- Gutters and downspouts offer adequate water damage

- A good drainage system

- The foundation, making sure it doesn't have any drainage issues

- The ground sloping away from the foundation

- Driveways and walkways that are even and not cracking

- Siding that's in good repair

- Trees, shrubbery, and plants don't look overgrown or unkempt

- Sprinkler systems properly working

- Decks and porches aren't decaying nor do they have any termite damage

- Steps and railings are secure

- Fireplaces' and chimneys' mortar isn't loose and crumbling

- Ceilings, walls, and floors aren't leaking

- Drywall isn't pulling away from interior walls

- Walls and ceilings don't have any cracks

- Floors aren't spongy or weak nor do they lean

- Doors and windows move smoothly and close properly

- Windows don't have evidence of mildew, moisture, or fog

- The garage's flooring isn't stained or cracked

- The garage's siding is in good condition

- Garage doors work properly

- The garage's foundation drains properly

- Soil slopes away from the garage

There are many things to look at and think about when buying and selling a house. This is why you should have a house inspection. Once you have these results, you can decide if the property is worth buying or how much to sell your house for. If you receive a bad inspection, you're helpless when it comes to whether or not the buyer will back out. However, if you're the one buying the house, you can try to buy the house for a lower price.

Throughout this time you need to keep your head up. Even if you receive a bad review this may not throw the buyer off because most of them expect to have to do some work anyway. If not, you should at least be able to reach a compromise that works for everyone. On the other hand, if you're planning on flipping the house, simply get some quotes on the work you need to do. With multiple bids, you can see how much it will take and use this to your benefit during negotiations.

Closing the Deal

You'll need to head into closing with this head up, positive thinking, "We can negotiate this" type of attitude. After all, closing day is a celebratory day. This is just a formality composed of signing paperwork, exchanging money, and shaking hands. However, you need to do some preparatory work to make sure it goes this way.

According to New York real estate attorney Neil Garfinkel communication is the key to success when it comes time for closing. So, a week before closing, talk to the people who represent you.

Stay on your loan officer or agent to make sure they have everything they need, including loan papers. It's also important to understand that by law you're allowed to check the closing settlement statement or the HUD-1 form 24 hours before closing. Make sure you take advantage of this time to compare the form to your good faith estimate (a.k.a. GFE form) that you received when you applied for your loan.

Make sure you have everything you're going to sign before signing it. This way you don't grow nervous when you go to closing and it's simply a matter of signing the papers and getting the keys. Also, by looking over the loan documents beforehand, you'll know exactly what to take with you to the closing.

Some of the items you'll typically need include:

- A certified check is definitely needed. While using a wire transfer is an option, typically this takes longer instead of being faster. This is because the closing won't happen until they actually have the wire confirmed. Depending on this timing, you could have a major problem.

- A photo ID

- Copies of your insurance policy for the property

- The GFE form, HUD-1 statement, or both in the event there are discrepancies

Even with all this planning, you won't know for certain if everything will go as planned and you'll get out of there in less than 30 minutes or things will go awry and you'll need more time. This is why you don't want to try to do this business on your lunch hour. Keep in mind delays are more likely if you're closing near the end of the month.

You also never know what will happen at the closing table. Some of the biggest holdups include:

- Double checking the numbers on the mortgage only to discover inconsistencies (e.g. correcting the interest rate or amount)

- A simple typo means the loan documents need sent back to the lender so they can redo them

This is why you should try to schedule your closing for earlier in the day. Also, you should never wait to the last day on your contract for holding your closing, especially if you're buying a foreclosed property or a short sale.

Chapter 6:
The Formula Behind Flipping

There are many strategies Realtors use today when selling houses. One of the most popular is the "99" strategy. This is when you sell your house for $499K instead of $500K. In doing so, the $1K you lose covers some of the buyer's closing costs, but the buyer thinks they're paying $500K. Ultimately this $1K doesn't mean much to you or the buyer, but there's a lot of strategy and psychology behind this.

Choosing Your Pricing Strategy

Ultimately, you need to listen carefully to your agent's pricing strategy because they know what will and what will not work. It's also important you understand that this isn't something you simply do then forget about. There are lots of factors you must consider, but you can't expect all of them, which is why you must stay flexible so you can quickly react to any change in market conditions or if you receive new information.

With this in mind, it's important to understand that there are four different types of pricing strategies you can use as a seller. These are:

- You don't want only one person interested in your house because real estate has some high stakes. If you price your house on the lower end of this range, you'll stimulate interest among several buyers. This works best if you're not in a big rush to sell the house.

- You want to make sure you know the price-point people typically search for when looking for a house in the neighborhood where your property is. This is important because if you list your house over that price-point and a Realtor creates and automated buyer search in their local database for properties under a set amount and you price your house slightly over that amount, it won't come up on their search. Unfortunately, this happens often.

- Never get "creative" with your asking price because this draws unnecessary attention to your house as if you'd painted the house purple. Buyers will want to know why you chose that figure, who the seller is, and so on. You want to stay as far in the background as possible, if not make yourself completely invisible. After all, your goal is to showcase your property and appeal to as many people as possible. If you get really quirky when it comes to your asking price, you'll contradict what is a "tried and true" strategy.

As you use one of these strategies and before you actually place your house on the market, make sure you work out a pricing contingency plan, especially if you want to try a higher price tag than you think you'll actually get. By having a "Plan B" you'll save yourself time and know what to expect if things don't work out with your original price tag.

The Importance of Considering Your Rehab Costs

You know you'll need to do a lot of work on your flip, but just how much is something you're probably wondering. When you've flipped a few houses, this is a number that's easier for you to know and understand (guessing repair costs within about 1 – 2% just from knowing the size and condition of the house) from the starting point, when you're just buying a house. However, if this is your first flip, there's a way of estimating the cost of your flip.

To estimate the cost of your repair costs, here are some helpful tips:

- Most houses in need of a "standard" cosmetic rehab will cost $20 per square foot. A "standard" rehab usually consists of all new flooring (carpet and tile or hardwood), paint (interior and exterior), baseboards, fixtures for both electric and plumbing, window treatments (blinds), doors, and some landscaping. So, if you buy a 1,500 sq. ft. house you'll spend around $30K on the rehab (1,500 x $20 = $30,000). Of course, if your house is a higher-end property, you'll need to spend $25 - $30 per square foot.

- Now adjust either up or down based on what else the house needs or what it doesn't need. For instance, if your house's kitchen is newly remodeled, you won't need to do anything more to it and you can remove the cost from your rehab costs. If you only need to repaint (interior and exterior) and redo the floors, you can do this for $2K - $5K. However, if you need to redo the roof, this typically costs $5K - $8K alone; a new HVAC system, $5K; new windows, $200 per window. Other things you may need to do include rewiring the electrical, redoing the plumbing, and structural requirements. Make sure you have this in mind when you come up with your first offer price, then when you have your offer accepted you and a licensed contractor can go through the property together to create a detailed "scope of work" and repair estimates just to make sure you didn't miss anything.

Estimating the Costs of Your Flip

One of this industry's biggest pitfalls comes from underestimating repair costs. Heed this warning! You're bound to come across unexpected repair costs when you flip a house, regardless how careful you are. This is because how much of the house you must fix can range from "almost nothing" to "almost everything.

With this checklist you can enter into a flip anticipating all the repair costs:

- The house itself: Does it need a simple cosmetic paint job? Do you need to change some fixtures? Do you need to gut the entire kitchen?

- The General Contractor: There's a good reason you want your general contractor involved from the start. Often, they know what you don't know about construction. Trying to do things without them will usually cost you more money than hiring them in the first place. You want a general contractor who knows what they're doing and will stick with your project until it's done.

- Subcontractors: These are the people who you'll turn to for specific repairs and fixes. They include painters, plumbers, and electricians. Your general contractor will help you get fair quotes from them, many general contractors will even find them for you.

- Carrying costs: Don't overlook these! You'll "own" the property for a few months. During that time you're responsible for the general upkeep of the property. This includes paying for utilities (e.g. gas, water, electric), insurance, and property taxes. Also, you may have to pay HOA or condo fees.

- Expecting the unexpected: Regardless of how careful you are, more than likely you'll come up with some surprises and their bill. You must always expect this to happen so you can build a buffer into the total amount you've estimated for repair costs. With this in mind, usually 10% over the number you've come up with is a good buffer.

Calculating Your Closing and Holding Expenses

When you watch house flipping shows, nobody ever seems to talk about closing and holding costs. You don't want all your profits sucked up in this way, so you do need to know about these things.

First, remember the closing costs. These are the buyer's closing costs, which are typically less than the selling closing costs. When you're buying a flip, you'll pay these costs. They're typically 0.5% of your purchasing price.

Secondly, don't forget sellers have closing costs too. These are the seller's closing costs and are somewhat more expensive than purchase closing costs. If you're using a Realtor, expect to pay them 5 – 6% commission. In certain areas and markets, your Realtor may also want you to pay for some of their expenses, which ranges from 1 – 6%, but typically is about 3%. So, make sure you include these percentages for closing costs.

Third, and finally, there are holding costs. Lots of people forget to think about these. However, you must still pay for things like property taxes, insurance, utilities, maintenance (e.g. lawn), and HOA while you "own" the house. Make sure you're aware of these expenses because depending on how long you hold on to the property, you'll have increased expenses.

Remembering Your Financing Costs

By now you're probably hoping there aren't any more expenses to think about. However, if you've used financing to buy your flip then you'll need to consider your financing costs. Obviously, this section doesn't apply to anyone who's using their own capital or have people they know financing the property.

Unfortunately, financing costs can really add up. Typically they work out to:

- A private money-lender: You'll pay between 8 – 12% annualized return on your capital.

- A hard money-lender: You'll pay a 12% annualized rate with extra (percentage) points and fees. Usually, your points are between 2 – 3 (2 – 3%) or about 1% per month you have the loan.

When you Don't Make Enough Money

Flipping houses is expensive. The expenses begin with acquiring the property. While there are lots people claiming low or no money financing, receiving these loans is difficult. So, if you must finance your acquisition, you must also pay interest. Don't forget this money is tax-deductible. However, this isn't a 100% deduction. So, every dollar you spend on interest adds to the amount of money you must earn when you sell the house so you break even on the deal.

Some people think by paying cash they'll get rid of the interest, but property holding costs still exist regardless of how you pay for the property itself. It's important you add these renovation costs into your closing price. When you plan to actually make a profit, you must make sure your sale price exceeds your cost of acquisition, cost of holding the property, and the cost of renovations combined.

Even if you manage to break even with these things, you still need to think about capital gains taxes. These still have a way of chipping away at your profit.

When you run out of Time

Renovating and flipping houses takes a lot of time. Initially, you spend months searching for the right property to buy. Once you own the house, you spend months rehabbing it before you can sell it. Don't forget during this time you must also schedule inspections to make sure the work you've done complies with the applicable building codes. If it doesn't, you'll need to spend more time and money to correct the issues. Then, finally, you'll need to invest more time into selling the property. If you choose to show your house yourself, this will take lots of time commuting and meeting with potential buyers.

Making a 10% profit on a $50K house results in a $5,000 profit. Some people think they're better off getting a good job whereby they'll earn this money in a few weeks or months from a steady paycheck without the time commitment and risk involved in flipping. This isn't meant to keep you from investing in flipping, but to make sure this is really what you want to do.

When you Don't Have Enough Skills or Knowledge

Professional builders, carpenters, and plumbers often flip houses on the side of their regular jobs because they have the knowledge, skills, and experience to find a house then fix it up and make some extra money. Of course, some of these people also work for unions that pay them an unemployment check throughout the winter months while they work on their flips. Regardless of how they do it, they understand that the real money made from house flipping is found in sweat equity. So, if you're good with a hammer, carpeting, hanging drywall, roofing, or install a kitchen sink, you have the necessary skills for flipping a house. However, if you have to pay a professional to do all this work for you, your profit margin will be dramatically reduced.

The same can also be said about knowledge because without it there's no way of choosing right property, in the right location, for the right price. Even if you get a great deal, you still need to know what renovations to make and which to forego. Regardless of the deal, there are also tax laws to understand and you also need to know when to cut your losses before your project turns into a money pit.

When you Don't Have Enough Patience

As a professional, you'll want to take your time and wait for the "perfect" property to avail itself to you. This is something most novices don't do, though. Instead, they rush out and buy the first property they see then hire the first contractor they find only to wonder why things are so expensive or take so long. Professionals don't run into this problem with contractors either because they pre-arrange them, ensuring they find ones who not only fit into their budget but also are reliable.

Once the house is ready for you to place it on the market for sale, you don't want to just hire any Realtor. This is what novices do, but as a professional, you'll want to at least give the FSBO model a good try. Doing so will lower your costs while maximizing your profits.

You can't rush through everything. It takes time for you to do everything. Unfortunately, sometimes your profit margin is slim while at other times you'll hit the jackpot.

Determining Sales Price and Your Profit

New investors typically want to know how much money they can make from flipping houses. This is because over the past decade many TV shows have shown flippers making great money. However, you should know that while some of these shows are realistic, others are somewhat contrived. Also, many of these shows give you the purchase price, rehab price, and the sales price. What they fail to show you are the other costs (e.g. closing costs, Realtor expenses, taxes, insurance, utilities, maintenance). You must consider those costs will you arrive at a realistic view of the profits.

It's also important to understand that you understand houses sell for different prices in different parts of the country. This pricing difference is also true about the various other expenses associated with rehabbing a house. Additionally, housing demand varies. The point here is the profit you make from flipping a house in Florida isn't the same as the profits you make from flipping a house in California nor will the cost of flipping a house in New Jersey be the same as the cost of flipping a house in Iowa.

You must also take into account other expenses as well, including taxes, insurance, utilities, and closing costs. These expenses vary depending on the state and even the house's neighborhood.

Additionally, it's interesting to note that in those areas where houses are lower priced, investors are more likely to pay for them in cash instead of taking out a loan. This makes sense when you think about the cost of financing, though. When you use cash to buy a house, you can maximize the flip's potential profit market since you won't have to pay any financing fees.

Setting up Your First Flip

What it really comes down to here is you want to think of flipping as a business. You already have a preconceived idea of how much money you'd like to earn. With this in mind, it's up to you to make those earnings a reality.

At the same time, flipping is also an investment. As such, you're bound to encounter risks along the way. It's up to you to decide, ahead of time, how much profit you need to make to make the risks worthwhile. Of course, you can lower your risk by using cash instead of depending on financing. You should also only buy a house you could rent if the market were to quickly turn soft. For instance, don't flip a pool house because if you can't sell it you don't want to rent this type of house. Also, remember pool houses come with high insurance costs.

Since you don't want to see your costs pile up, it's important you're ready to start working on your flip immediately after closing. This means buying all your materials and scheduling your contractors for that day because you want to make sure you rehab your flip as fast as possible. Each day your property remains unsold eats up your profit in the form of taxes, insurance, utilities, and maintenance.

Conclusion

Thank you again for buying this book! I hope this book helped you to start your flipping business. While there are so many things involved in a profitable flip, you now have the tools to make yours happen. The next step is to go ahead and buy your first property.

This is an exciting time for you! Don't get overwhelmed with the various steps involved in your first flip. Remember! Everything you need is right here in this book, so when you start feeling overwhelmed, go back and read through things again.

Finally, if you enjoyed this book please consider check out our Amazon Author Page at https://www.amazon.com/-/e/B01LYIFPLO

Here you will find all you need to know about Rental Property Investing, Real Estate Sales, Real Estate Investing, REITs, Credit Score Repair, and even Tiny House Living if that's something you fancy!! If you check out our Real Estate Library, you are guaranteed to profit from Real Estate Investing and turn this into a lucrative income stream for the rest of your life. Don't miss out!!

Last but certainly not least, if you found this book useful in anyway, a review on Amazon is always appreciated! You can write a review on our book's page which can be accessed through this link:

https://www.amazon.com/Flipping-Houses-Comprehensive-Beginners-Properties-ebook/dp/B01MQCR3OP/

Thank you and good luck!

www.ingramcontent.com/pod-product-compliance
Lightning Source LLC
Chambersburg PA
CBHW070406190526
45169CB00003B/1131